A Perfect Chord

Melanie Lotfali

Indi-bird loved to sing.

She knew how to sing one note.

She sang it beautifully

and with all her heart.

One day Jarrah-bird
came to visit.
He also knew how
to sing one note.
They sang together.

Attracted by the sound,
Tai-bird landed on the branch.
He also knew how to sing
just one note.

It was different from the others.
He added his note
to the chord.

Marama-bird heard the beautiful harmony of the three different notes.

"I can sing a note too," she chirped.
She joined the group.

Tama-bird flew in with a
long loud "Cheeeeep Cheeeep".
Joyfully he added his note
to the music.

The harmony of the different notes was like a magnet for Mihi and Skye. They glided over to the branch. They opened their beaks and sang their notes. Each bird's note was different from the others. Each note was beautiful. Together they made the perfect chord.

The diversity in the human family should be the cause of love and harmony, as it is in music where many different notes blend together in the making of a perfect chord.

~ Bahá'í Writings ~

Copyright © 2013 Melanie Lotfali

A Perfect Chord
by Melanie Lotfali is licensed
under a Creative Commons
Attribution-NonCommercial-ShareAlike 4.0
International License.

ISBN 978-0-9945817-9-2

www.ingramcontent.com/pod-product-compliance
Lightning Source LLC
Chambersburg PA
CBHW061938290426
44113CB00025B/2950